Awfully Wedded

Also by Elissa Stein and Daniel Mailliard

Chunks: A Barfology
Tales from the Prom (with Daniel Mailliard)

Awfully Wedded

Tales of Disaster from the Big Day

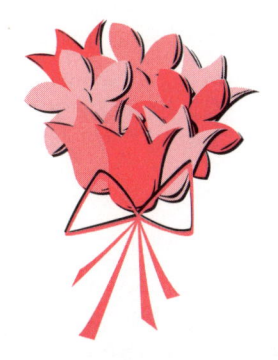

Elissa Stein and Daniel Mailliard

St. Martin's Griffin
New York

Daniel dedicates this book to Dawn Drazdys—his favorite dancing partner at weddings.

Elissa dedicates this book to the fabulous Miss Iz, who will one day grow up and be horribly embarrassed by the silly books her mom did; to Jon, who handles her projects with tremendous aplomb; and to Erica, who will be writing books of her own one day.

AWFULLY WEDDED: TALES OF DISASTER FROM THE BIG DAY. Copyright © 1999 by Elissa Stein and Daniel Mailliard. All rights reserved. Printed in the United States of America. No part of this book may be used or reproduced in any manner whatsoever without written permission except in the case of brief quotations embodied in critical articles or reviews. For information, address St. Martin's Press, 175 Fifth Avenue, New York, N.Y. 10010

Design by Elissa Stein
Illustrations by Chris Murphy and Elissa Stein

Library of Congress Cataloging-in-Publication Data

Awfully wedded : tales of disaster from the big day / [compiled by] Elissa Stein and Daniel Mailliard.
    p.   cm.
  ISBN 0-312-20847-2 (pbk.)
  1. Weddings Humor.   I. Stein, Elissa.   II. Mailliard, Daniel.
PN6231.W37A94   1999
392.5'02'07—dc21   99-25092
                                                        CIP

First St. Martin's Griffin Edition: June 1999

10 9 8 7 6 5 4 3 2 1

Intro

It's the biggest day of your life. All the money, all the planning, all the relatives you never even knew you had. It's your wedding day. And just like the couples involved in the ceremony, most weddings are disasters waiting to happen.

But why cry over spilt champagne, complain about the seating arrangements, or bitch about the divorce rate when you can laugh at somebody else's expense.

Here's to some of the most disastrous weddings recorded in modern times. From television to the movies, from weddings in the news to the weddings of people we know, *Awfully Wedded* tackles the big questions like: What do you do when the groom has sex with a man the day of your wedding; what do you do when your mother has a heart attack on the way to the ceremony; and what do you do with that god-awful, you-can-never-wear-it-again bridesmaid dress you've just spent three hundred dollars on?

The perfect gift for a bride-to-be or a recent divorcée, *Awfully Wedded* is a celebration of what could go wrong and did.

Arlene

a guest with a ringside seat

My friend Marie's daughter got married several years ago. They had a lovely wedding and a huge reception—I believe there were over three hundred people there.

During the ceremony it was hard to miss one of the bridesmaids carrying on with one of the ushers. They walked down the aisle together, holding hands, whispering and giggling. During the ceremony they kept smiling at each other and when we got to the reception, they sat next to each other on the dais. We all thought they were an adorable couple, they must have been newlyweds.

She was. He wasn't. She had been married to someone else for five months. By the time she and the usher got up to dance together the husband came storming across the dance floor, ready for a fight.

Marie's great-aunt Sophia quickly got up and ran over to intervene, but instead of stopping the fight, got in the middle of it—she caught the punch intended for the usher and crumpled to the floor, out cold. Someone called 911 and an ambulance arrived, whisking Aunt Sophia to the hospital.

She suffered a cracked cheekbone but recovered pretty quickly. Not as quickly as the bridesmaid and her husband. They got divorced.

Susan

a guest who thought you really could wear it again

I've been a bridesmaid several times, and while all the brides say "I hope you get to wear the dress again," we all know it's not likely to ever happen. Except once. . . .

I had been dating this guy David for about three months when he asked me to go with him to his cousin's wedding in New Jersey. I barely knew him and figured I'd never see these relatives again, so I decided to wear a bridesmaid's outfit from a wedding I was just in. I swear, I've never done this before—it's just that I really didn't want to spend money on a new dress. It was a long, fuchsia, two-piece outfit and I didn't think I'd look too bad.

As the ceremony started and the first bridesmaid walked down the aisle, I thought I'd die. She was wearing my dress. Same color. Same everything. Then five more girls came down the aisle, looking just like me. I just sat there, mortified, knowing the rest of the night was going to be an embarrassing disaster.

We had no choice; we had to walk down the reception line. Several of the bridesmaids giggled when they saw me, but the bride was not amused. Here I was, a total stranger, looking like I belonged in her wedding party.

For the rest of the night I had to fight the photographers who kept insisting I was needed for photo sessions.

Not only that, I ended up marrying David, so I see these people regularly. It's a story that will never go away.

Dawn
a bride on pins and needles

My bridesmaids were late and I was getting really pissed. It was the morning of my wedding and I was sitting in the basement of my church, frantically pacing up and down, cursing and blowing cigarette smoke out of one of the stained-glass windows when the first one finally showed up. After I screamed at her for five straight minutes, she explained to me that the woman who was making their dresses never finished them—she had to redesign all the dresses for a wedding that took place before mine and never caught up.

Susan, the first girl to show up, had her hem pinned. Molly, the next girl to arrive, had her hem and right sleeve pinned. Kelly, girl-number-three, had a pinned hem and two pinned sleeves. The next two bridesmaids were even worse. They showed up to church ten minutes apart, each dress with more pinning and less sewing.

While they were trying to get dressed, my mother ran around with a box of Band-Aids, helping the girls who cut themselves and making sure there were no bloodstains on the pink satin. She had the photographer stop taking pictures of me and start taking evidence photos of the dresses for the lawsuit I was surely going to file after the ceremony.

Things didn't get much better at the reception. The more we all drank, the more we all danced. The more we all danced, the more the dresses fell apart. Several of the men at my reception danced for the first times in their lives, hoping that a vital part of a bridesmaid's dress would come unpinned during the song. By the end of the reception, the bridesmaids had to borrow T-shirts and boxers from their dates because their dresses were in pieces on the floor.

And on the way home, they all piled into a limo and went to the bank, stopping payment on the checks to the dressmaker.

Sal
a finicky guest

I wasn't going to go to this wedding reception because I was on a diet and didn't want to be tempted to eat. But the bride caught my eye at the wedding and I knew she'd kill me if I didn't go to the reception. It was a catered affair and everything looked great, but I vowed I would not eat. And it was a good thing I did because, toward the end of the reception, over 75 percent of the guests had to be taken away in ambulances because of food poisoning. A pasta salad with fish oil was the culprit; there were so many victims that they had to be taken to several hospitals throughout the city because one emergency room couldn't handle them all.

Tom
a bewildered guest

A friend of mine from work was getting married in Chinatown and I decided it would be a nice gesture if I went. I was given directions to the wedding hall and schlepped all the way down to Chinatown with present in hand. When I got there I noticed that I was the only white person in the entire congregation. The congregation also noticed that I was the only white person there, and whispers and rumblings in Chinese went rolling through the chapel. I didn't see anyone from work, but then again, I was new to the department and didn't know a lot of people.

I also didn't know my friend's bride, so when an unfamiliar Asian woman came walking down the aisle I didn't think anything of it. In fact, I didn't think anything was wrong until the groom stepped out from behind a screen. It was not my friend. I was in the wrong wedding chapel at the wrong wedding and the only way out was down the center aisle.

I waited until the bride got to the end of the aisle, and the bridesmaids all got situated, then I excused myself, climbed over the three people at the end of the pew, and walked down the center aisle to the back of the chapel.

Whispers and rumblings in Chinese again filled the chapel, and only got louder as I began rummaging through the gift table looking for my gift. Finally I found what looked like my present and walked out of the chapel just as two big guys were walking toward me. I'm sure they thought I was stealing the present.

I reread the directions my friend had given me and decided if I couldn't find the right chapel, I'd just go straight to the reception. I was thirty minutes early, but that just gave me more time to drink. As the guests arrived I got nervous because none of them looked familiar, but finally some people I knew started showing up and the reception went off without a hitch.

A couple weeks later my friend and his new bride sent me a thank-you note for the lovely Tiffany candlesticks. . . . I laughed out loud as I read the note, thinking to myself that I must have picked up the wrong present—what I had bought them was a cheese plate.

Rosemary
a bride with a controlling jewish mother

It's a Jewish tradition: When you get married, the groom breaks a glass. It symbolizes good luck for the couple. Instead of a glass, most people use a lightbulb, so that it'll break easily on the first try.

At my wedding, it took six tries for my husband to break the glass. When the cloth around it was removed, we saw it was a solid highball glass, not a lightbulb. To this day, I think my mom wasn't thrilled I was marrying him and this was her way of putting a jinx on things.

in the movies

Private Benjamin

The day Judy married Yale she got everything she ever wanted: a big house, a live-in maid, two walk-in closets, and a successful businessman to take care of her. Too bad she only had it for six hours. On her wedding night, after already being serviced by Judy in the back of the limo during the reception, Yale dies while going back for seconds (and we're not talking about the buffet).

The distraught Judy, unforgettably played by Goldie Hawn, doesn't know what to do. Her first marriage lasted only six months and her second only six hours. Miserable, and sure she is being punished by God, rich-girl Judy disappears from her dead husband's funeral and hides out in a hotel suite.

Alone for the first time in her life, Judy calls a radio talk show for advice. Unfortunately for Judy, Frasier wasn't on the air then, and she ends up talking to an army recruiter, who apparently gets paid by the numbers. He cons Judy into joining the army with the promise of yachts, condos, and $428 per month.

But green doesn't seem to be Judy's color. She screws up and screws around until she gets her entire platoon punished—marching in circles during a rainstorm with Judy announcing, "I want to wear my sandals again, I want to go out to lunch, I want to be normal."

Sadly, Judy isn't normal. Because when her father and mother come to break her out of the army, she suddenly doesn't want to go. Despite her controlling father and horrific drill sergeant, Captain Louis, Judy decides to stay in the army and be all she can be.

Finishing basic training at the top of her class, Judy gets assigned to an elite parachute force, the Thornbirds. But on the day of her big jump, she can't make the leap of faith and backs down. Her commander, "Thorny," lets her off the hook, informing her that there are other ways she can serve. He then pops off his parachute and starts unbuttoning his shirt. Judy's only escape: out the plane and into the wild blue yonder.

Back on ground, old Thorny tries to exile Judy to Greenland so she can't ruin his reputation. "Penguins," Judy replies, "I don't think so." Guam means malaria and the South Pacific means her hair will frizz. So where does Judy end up? Paris, and in the arms of Henri (Armand Assante).

They had met in New Orleans while Judy was on leave, and after Judy pops in on him in France they quickly become lovers. . . . Well, Henri, Judy, the maid, and Henri's last girlfriend (oh, those French). Despite Henri's wandering eye, Judy moves in with him, and when forced to choose between him and the army (Henri was a Communist for a short time) she chooses him (and his really big house).

Once on track, Judy slips back into her old ways. She becomes more of Henri's maid than his lover, taking his car to the shop, picking up his dry cleaning, and having his dog neutered (she should have taken Henri instead).

But this is what Judy has always wanted, right? Maybe not. As she walks down the aisle in a pilgrimlike wedding dress, her once-blond hair now flaming red at Henri's request, Judy begins to flash back to her marriage with Yale. As Henri says his vows, Judy flashes to her controlling father, and as Henri is about to slip the ring onto her finger, Judy snaps out of it.

"Not so fast," she says, and, admitting that the timing is bad, she breaks up with Henri. It's not what she wants after all. She doesn't need a man to make her whole. And when Henri says she's stupid for feeling this way she punches him in the face and walks out of the ceremony.

Once outside, Judy rips off her veil and lets it fly in a sudden wind that can only be described as a cleansing breath. Judy spins on her heel and walks defiantly and independently down the driveway (hopefully to the nearest drug store to get some Miss Clairol for that awful hair).

Alicia

an overheated guest

My husband's boss invited us to his super-expensive, posh, celebrity-studded wedding at a fancy New York City hotel. We got there half an hour early, were served champagne, and seated in a room absolutely filled with beautiful white and yellow flowers. I noticed that the flowers were starting to wilt and the room was stifling—someone said there was an air-conditioning problem.

The ceremony started late and by the time the first bridesmaid started down the aisle, we were all dripping wet. Suddenly there was a murmur and then a commotion behind us to the left. An older man had passed out. A waiter rushed in with ice water. When the old man came to the ceremony started again. Then, (I swear this is true) another old man passed out. This seemed to be more serious: He didn't revive right away and the room got a little out of control. Hotel security came rushing in, knocking over a huge flowered arch that framed the entrance. It went crashing down on the three back rows of people and they all started screaming.

Then the groom crumpled. Really. The paramedics arrived and split up to aid the old man and the groom. The old man was taken away on a stretcher (he turned out to be okay) and the groom had an oxygen mask strapped to his face. Everyone ran out the back, to cooler air and away from disaster.

Finally, with things somewhat settled down, dinner was served and the reception began—only, someone realized that the ceremony had never been completed. After the main course the rabbi grabbed the band's microphone and concluded the ceremony. He then led the horah, announced the cutting of the cake, and sang a couple of songs with the band.

We had never seen anything like that before. Although, to tell the truth, we had never seen anything like that entire wedding before either.

Marianne
a pooper-scooping bride

It was the second marriage for both of us so we decided to have a wedding that would really make us happy. We loved the water and planned our ceremony to take place at sunrise, on a dock, by a lake in Maine. We invited only close friends and relatives, and our beagle, Molly.

The sun started to rise; the reflection over the water was beautiful. As the ceremony was about to begin, I noticed the priest looking a little concerned. He looked at me and then back down at his feet: There was poop all over the dock. Molly had made herself right at home.

My father found a shovel in a shack back at the beach, cleaned up the mess, and kept Molly on a leash for the rest of the morning.

Cliff
a scorched DJ

I was a DJ for a Long Island wedding hall for several years. I saw several crazy things, but nothing more outrageous than when the bride's dress caught on fire.

The dinner plates were just being cleared when the waiters at the hall brought out dessert: flaming cherries jubilee. The crowd was really impressed and began to clap for the waiters; then the one serving the bride and groom got a little cocky. He stopped and bowed to the crowd before putting his tray on the table, and while he was bowing, his arm caught on fire. He panicked and threw the still-flaming dessert into the bride's lap and her dress caught on fire.

The groom put the fire out by pouring a pitcher of water onto his new wife. The waiter was fired, no one ate their dessert, and for the first song of the night we were tempted to play "Burning Down the House," but instead we went with the bride's selection of "Sunrise, Sunset."

The Brady Bunch

Here's a story of a lovely lady, who was planning a wedding of her own. . . . You know the story, but do you remember the ceremony?

Carol Martin, who has three girls of her own, is marrying Mike Brady, who has three boys and a dog. What we don't find out in the opening credits is that Carol had a cat and that Fluffy and Tiger would be attending the wedding.

In the middle of their beautiful ceremony (Carol's lemon-yellow dress matched the tablecloths), Fluffy meowed, Tiger escaped from the car, and a chase ensued. The two animals, followed by Greg, Marcia, Peter, Jan, Bobby, Cindy, and Alice, ran down the aisle, through rows of guests, and across the buffet table, knocking over food, drink, and finally the wedding cake—right on top of Mike and Carol.

The ceremony ruined, Mike and Carol (even though they had taken tranquilizers before the wedding) yelled at the kids for bringing the animals and then left on their honeymoon. But these were America's perfect parents, and neither one could enjoy the honeymoon knowing that they yelled at their kids.

So what's a newly wedded couple to do? If you're the Brady bunch you go home, get the kids, get the maid, get the dog, get the cat, and invite them all to go on the honeymoon with you. No wonder there was never a seventh Brady.

Ava
a nervous bridesmaid

My sister got a phone call from a high school friend she hadn't spoken to in years, asking her to be a bridesmaid at her wedding. Ellen, caught totally off guard, said yes. She regretted her answer as soon as she hung up, but it was too late. So she dealt with it by not dealing—she went to her dress fittings but that was about it. She even blew off the rehearsal dinner.

The morning of the wedding, she got dressed in her peach-satin, hoop-skirted, to-the-floor gown with matching gloves and hat. I have to say she looked pretty ridiculous and she knew it. She begged me to come to the church with her for moral support.

We got to the church only to find out it was a Long Island blowout wedding for four hundred. Ellen, who hates crowds and doesn't like anyone looking at her (at almost six feet tall she was towering over the entire wedding party), was really nervous. I left her looking pale and sort of shaking.

As she walked down the aisle, I noticed a slight quiver in her upper lip. By the time she got to the front of the church she had a twitch she couldn't control. The other bridesmaids, the ushers, even the minister were watching Ellen's face contort into an ugly Elvis snarl. It was fascinating to watch but also really uncomfortable. She tried hiding behind her flowers, which only made more people stare. By the time she finally walked back down the aisle, people were whispering and pointing.

She locked herself in the bathroom and refused to come out. I diverted the photographer and we made our getaway—never to speak to the bride again.

in the movies

Sixteen Candles

This movie just goes to prove our point—being a bridesmaid is the most thankless job in the world. After the fact, no one remembers who we were, what we wore, or what we looked like—except us.

In *Sixteen Candles*, Molly (she was never better than this) Ringwald plays one of two bridesmaids in her older sister's wedding—they both wear light lilac dresses with flowered wreaths in their hair and ribbons flowing down their backs. But in a ceremony like this, it's no wonder we're the only ones paying attention to the bridesmaids.

The bride, you see, takes not one, not two, but four muscle relaxants right before the ceremony—she had just gotten her period and was cramping, a fact accidently announced to the entire church by the bride's father, right after she passes out.

When they finally get her back on her feet, the bridesmaids come running down the aisle, while the tiny woman from *Poltergeist* plays "Here Comes the Bride." And here she comes. On the short way down the aisle she makes fun of two guests' hats, thanks people for their gifts, and then stops halfway down to rest. She also throws her veil onto the altar because it keeps sticking to her tongue and she can't say her vows.

After the ceremony, while the bride is stripping out of her slip and flirting with the limo driver, the oft-forgotten Ringwald goes back in the church to recover the discarded veil. When she comes back with it, the entire wedding party has already left for the reception.

Don't feel too bad, though. The boy of her dreams—with perfect hair, perfect cheekbones, perfect eyebrows, perfect teeth, perfect clothes, and a perfect red Porsche 924—is there instead. With very little convincing, Ringwald decides to skip the reception and share a romantic, candlelit kiss with her new, perfect boyfriend on top of a perfect glass table inside his perfect house.

The evening turns out out to be—you guessed it—perfect, and the candlelit room even seems to make the purple bridesmaid dress look good. Not perfect, but good.

3o

a groom on the run

I was married pretty young, at a time when I still had the ol' college party spirit. The two nights before the wedding were spent on a nonstop eating and drinking binge. I woke up on Sunday morning with a hangover, a sick stomach, and a serious case of the jitters. It was the hottest day of the year at 96 degrees, and I didn't know it at the time but I was also coming down with the flu. But perhaps I'll save that for the book about nightmare honeymoons.

By the time my best man got me together and into his car we were late. The aforementioned factors and the thought of all those relatives was really unsettling my digestive system, and the mad dash down Fifth Avenue to the temple didn't help. I was getting married at the largest and richest temple in New York.

We got there minutes before the ceremony was to start, but I figured I still had a couple of moments to get myself together (find a bathroom) in the relative comfort of the temple. To my surprise the temple did not have air conditioning and the rabbi's robing room where I was to "freshen up" looked like it hadn't been renovated since the last World War.

Of course, I really didn't care: At that moment all I needed was to adjust the plumbing a bit. I found the bathroom, threw myself down on the seat, and let nature take its course. Incredibly, although tickets to the high holy days cost one thousand dollars a pop, the toilet paper dispenser was the kind they had in elementary school when you were in kindergarten! You know, the metal box that hung on the wall with the individual folded squares, which you pulled out one by one and which had a slit in the front to let you know how many were left. I, of course, had bigger things to be concerned about at the time and the only reason I so vividly recall this particular aspect of my wedding day was that when I pulled down the first square, it was not followed by a second. The second square remained hidden inside the box, and although it, and several others, were clearly visible through the slotted window, my fingers were too big to reach into the slot and, try as I might, that single square just did not do the job.

My best man started to call for me to come out, insisting that everyone was waiting and that Grampa was about to pass out from the heat. I don't really know what went through my head next, but suddenly I grabbed the underside of the box and with almost superhuman strength I pried the bottom of the dispenser sufficiently open with my fingers to reach the priceless commodity inside.

With the last vestiges of my fading strength I made it down the aisle and managed to get married without further incident.

in the movies

In & Out

It was going to be the perfect wedding. Kevin Klein, a tidy, well-mannered, English professor is going to marry the girl of his dreams—Joan Cusack, who, with help from Richard Simmons, lost almost eighty pounds for the occasion.

Kevin's mom (perfectly portrayed by Debbie Reynolds) has waited her whole life for this day, and Kevin's father, the curmudgeonly Wilford Brimley is coming in from the fields for the day.

The only problem: Kevin is gay. One week before the wedding, Kevin's former student Matt Dillon outs Kevin during his Academy Award speech.

A media blitz ensues, and tabloid journalist Tom Selleck comes to town to do an exposé on Kevin, who, in the meantime, is denying his homosexuality.

But let's face it, he knows all the words to *Funny Girl*, *Funny Lady,* and *Yentl*. Kevin is also, as we stated before, a well-mannered, tidy English professor, so of course he has to be gay.

And Tom Selleck, who's gay himself, is going to prove it. After almost running Kevin off the road (earth-conscious gay man that he is, Kevin rides a bike to work), Tom kisses Kevin full on the lips for a very long time.

Stirred, but not shaken, Kevin continues to deny he's gay, right up to the day of the wedding. As Joan Cusack comes walking down the aisle in a huge, white dress that puts the eighty pounds she lost right back on, Kevin admits to her, and the entire congregation, that he is in fact gay.

Joan punches Kevin, Kevin's mother passes out, and Tom Selleck calls the nearest hotel to try and book a room.

Catching wind of the trouble he has caused, Matt Dillon comes back to town to "straighten" everything out.

He meets Joan, another former teacher of his, who is running around the town in her wedding dress looking for a straight man, and they fall in love (the authors of the book disagree here). Tom and Kevin, it seems, are also in love (for now), and Kevin's mom and dad are in love as well, which they prove by renewing their vows and finally giving Kevin's mom the wedding she's always dreamed of having.

on TV

Bewitched

It's the typical boy-meets-girl story with one small twist: She's a witch. In the pilot episode, Darrin and Samantha run into each other in a department store and fall instantly in love.

But all isn't champagne and silk teddies for Darrin and Samantha, because Sam's mother, Endora, shows up on the honeymoon. She tries to convince Sam to come home with her, but Sam's a witch in love and there's just no changing her mind. Endora will change Darrin into a monkey, a statue, and an old man, but she'll never change Sam's mind.

Endora supposes that as soon as Darrin finds out Sam's a witch the marriage will be over, but Darrin is not so easily scared. He tells Sam he loves her no matter what, but also tells her she can never use her witchcraft, then he sends her into the kitchen to make dinner. But Darrin can't keep Sam in the kitchen forever.

A jealous ex-girlfriend decides to throw a dinner party in honor of the happy couple. At the party, the ex does everything she can to embarrass Sam. But while the ex is a bitch, the wife is a witch, and Sam's not about to be outdone by a mere mortal.

With her famous twitch of the nose, Sam knocks the girlfriend's hair out of place, sticks a huge piece of spinach to her teeth, drops a tray of food in her lap, and blows her hairpiece right off. After the party, Sam confesses that giving up witchcraft may be just a little harder than she thought.

Eric

a lifesaving guest

Some friends of ours got married in the Ozarks—a bunch of lakes in the Midwest. We were staying on one island and had to take a boat to another island, where the ceremony was being held.

Since we didn't know most of the other guests, our group of friends sat outside on the top of the boat, while everyone else went down below.

We were all drinking, but it seemed like the downstairs guests were really partying hard. One girl came up top, babbled something incoherently and passed out.

It wasn't that long a boat ride. We all kind of wondered how much she really could have had to drink, so we went down to see what was going on and found everyone below passed out.

Apparently something was wrong with the boat, and carbon monoxide was filling the bottom cabin. We pulled all the guests out of the cabin into the fresh air and had the boat's pilot pull over at the nearest dock to get medical help. Ambulances were called and all the sick guests were taken to the hospital.

When the bride and groom heard what had happened, they rushed to the hospital and never had the ceremony. They ended up getting married the next day over lunch.

Carolyn
a superstitious bride

They say there will be seven signs that announce the end of the world. No one told me about the five signs foretelling a bad marriage.

The restaurant at which my boyfriend asked me to "go steady" burned to the ground two weeks after I said yes. Sign number one.

My boyfriend then proposed to me during a dinner cruise in New York harbor. A month later, the boat sank to the bottom of the harbor. Sign number two.

Two words can describe the day of the wedding—Hurricane Hugo. Sign number three.

The morning of the wedding my fiancé's sister (a bridesmaid) called to say that she was running late: She had to take their grandmother to the hospital—she couldn't breathe. Sign number four.

And then, as my mom climbed into the limo on our way to the church, she fell onto the car floor clutching her chest. My father yelled for the driver to take us to the hospital, but my mother, determined to get me married off, ignored her heart attack and insisted that we go to the church instead. Sign number five.

Denying the signs and my gut reaction that I was heading for disaster, I got married anyway.

It lasted a total of thirteen months and thirteen days, and ended when my husband got another woman pregnant while still married to me.

David

a flaming altar boy
(not that kind of flaming)

I was an altar boy all through grade school primarily because it got me out of classes, but it was also a good way to make a little extra money. If you worked a wedding or a funeral, the families were pretty good about thanking you with cash, but there was one wedding I didn't get thanked for at all.

I was working the wedding of a family friend and my mom was one of the several hundred wedding guests. There were flowers at the entrance of the church, at the end of each pew, and even on the altar. The pollen was so thick you could see it in the air. It was also beginning to make me really tired.

I guess I wasn't paying attention to what I was doing, because in the middle of the wedding my mother jumped up and screamed, "David, you're on fire!" I looked down and saw that one of the altar candles had caught my robe on fire. The next thing I knew the priest was throwing me to the ground trying to put me out.

I went to the hospital to have my minor burns looked at while the bride and groom, unhappy that their perfect wedding didn't go over exactly as planned, went to the reception.

in the movies

Four Weddings and a Funeral

It's easier if we just bullet-point this one:

Wedding #1

- The blond bride looks like a huge meringue.

- Andie MacDowell arrives with a huge, I mean huge, black hat on.

- Hugh Grant (the best man) forgets the rings and leaves in the middle of the ceremony to borrow a huge (I mean huge) plastic heart ring and metal skull-and-crossbones ring.

- Hippies sing James Taylor at the ceremony.

- Kristin Scott Thomas flirts with a priest-in-training (Mr. Bean) at the reception.

- Hugh Grant, stammering, inadvertently tells a guy his wife is sleeping with another man, throws up, then sleeps with Andie MacDowell, who leaves him first thing in the morning.

- Bernard and Lydia make out, which leads to . . .

Wedding #2

- Bernard and Lydia get married.

- Scarlett (a bridesmaid) walks down the aisle with the back of her dress unzipped and her blue Jockey underwear showing.

- The priest-in-training that Kristin Scott Thomas flirted with is now the bumbling priest presiding over the ceremony using such phrases as the "Holy Goat," "Awfully Wedded," and "The Father, the Son, and the Holy Spigot."

- Andie MacDowell runs into Hugh and announces that she's engaged. He stammers.

- An old woman asks Kristin Scott Thomas if she's a lesbian, and Kristin announces that no, she's, in fact, in love with Hugh . . . then confesses to being a lesbian once for fifteen minutes at boarding school.

- Hugh gets stuck at a table with four of his old girlfriends (including one called Duckface) who all decide to compare notes on him over coffee.

- Hugh escapes to the bridal suite where he is forced to hide in a closet when the bride and groom break in and start having sex.

- Scarlett explains the concept of "boinking" to a ten-year-old flower girl.

- Andie invites Hugh up to her room for a nightcap and sleeps with him again (then tells him she's slept with thirty-three different men including a ménage with a father-and-son duo—I ask you, is this a girl you'd want to marry?).

Wedding #3

- Andie gets married to an old Scottish guy.
- The wedding party wears kilts.
- Scarlett meets Chester, a hunky American from Texas.
- Kristin tells Hugh she loves him. Hugh stammers.
- Gareth has a heart attack and dies (hence the funeral).

Wedding #4

- Hugh decides to marry Duckface.
- Tom meets his second cousin twice-removed and hears thunderbolts.
- Andie shows up and announces she's divorced (probably got caught sleeping with the help).
- Hugh has second thoughts and stammers to the priest, his brother, and his best man.
- David (Hugh's hunky deaf brother) stops the wedding and announces, in sign language, that Hugh is in love with someone else.
- The priest asks Hugh if he loves someone else and he replies "I do."
- Duckface punches Hugh in the nose.
- Hugh bleeds.
- In the end, Andie shows up at Hugh's house and they decide not to get married. (Oh, they're going to live together in sin for the rest of their lives and have a baby, they're just not going to bother getting married.)

Carol

a bride under a black cloud

My husband and I have been married for over fifty years.

We wanted our wedding to be very romantic. We got married on Valentine's Day and planned a lovely reception.

The flowers were beautiful, the band wonderful, and the wedding cake was breathtaking. It was four layers high and on top, instead of the traditional bride and groom, we had a cage with two lovebirds.

When it was time to cut the cake, one of the waiters took the birdcage off. As Nate and I made the first cut, we heard a commotion behind us. Somehow the door to the cage opened and the birds came rushing out, flying quickly to the top of the room. Next thing we know, bird poop landed on the floor right next to me. Guests started ducking for cover as the birds flew and pooped, and pooped and flew, all over the room. People were hiding under tables, covering their heads with napkins and suit jackets.

With that, the party was over. No one knew what to do or how to get the birds down. Our day of romance turned into a day of hit or miss.

And then, apparently, it turned into a day of tragedy. The next morning, someone found the birds in a corner. One had pecked the other to death.

Helpful Hints to Avoid Disaster

Weddings today come in so many shapes and sizes. Not only can so many things go wrong at weddings, so many things do. In an effort to keep your wedding disaster-free, the authors suggest these simple steps to follow, so you're prepared for any wedding scenario.

Vertically challenged wedding

- ☑ Avoid lining the aisle with yellow flowers—it might suggest the yellow brick road.
- ☑ No matter how great the bandleader is, stop him before he gets to the limbo.
- ☑ Make sure the flower girl is shorter than the bride.

An overweight couple

- ☑ Make sure you're not last in the buffet line.
- ☑ Don't ask the bride where she got her dress*es*.
- ☑ Instead of dancing you'll be sweatin' to the oldies.

Interfaith wedding

☑ Catholics light the unity candle—primarily to make the ceremony longer.

☑ Jews stand under a chuppah—a lovely job for any florist.

☑ Indians paint their hands with henna—long before Madonna did

Gay wedding

☑ Avoid asking which one is the bride and which is the groom.

☑ Give cash—they have better taste than you do.

☑ His and His towels are an inappropriate gift.

Underage wedding

☑ Forget the guest registry, just sign their yearbooks.

☑ Forgo giving a gift, contribute to their college fund instead.

☑ BYOB.

Pregnant bride

☑ Take all photos from the waist up.

☑ Don't wrap your wedding gift in Barney wrapping paper.

☑ To compensate for morning sickness, have a late afternoon wedding.

A "May/December" wedding

- ☑ Thank God Tony Bennett is back.
- ☑ Have the wedding at night—soft lighting is eminently more flattering.
- ☑ Don't ask about a prenup, don't ask about a will.

Second wedding

- ☑ Toss on something you already have in the closet.
- ☑ Serve leftovers.
- ☑ Re-gift.

When the bride and the groom are related

- ☑ Monograms make it easy.
- ☑ There is no "Bride's side/Groom's side."
- ☑ Incest is best!

White-trash wedding

- ☑ They call it a wedding cake, you call it Sara Lee.
- ☑ Don't ask when the due date is.
- ☑ When in doubt—the higher the hair, the closer to heaven.

Greek wedding

- ☑ Avoid giving good china—they're just going to throw it anyway.
- ☑ Bring No-Doz—it's a long-ass ceremony.
- ☑ Keep your napkin clean, you'll need it later for dancing.

Italian wedding

- ☑ They aren't bodyguards, they're "members of the wedding party."
- ☑ Don't ask about Uncle Joe.
- ☑ Eat. Eat more.

Irish wedding

- ☑ Don't bother bringing a gift, they'll be too drunk to remember.
- ☑ A claddauh ring is not a secret unit of the IRA.
- ☑ Don't worry if a fight breaks out—plenty of cops at this wedding.

Jewish wedding

☑ When they say they're honeymooning in the homeland, they're not talking about Long Island.

☑ Diamonds really are a girl's best friend—and she got them wholesale.

☑ Mazel tov is not a cocktail.

Two lawyers

☑ Expect the vows to be followed by disclaimers.

☑ If you trip or fall at the reception don't worry— you'll have a case.

☑ The suits they're discussing aren't Armani, the suits they're wearing are.

Two doctors

☑ Set your pagers to vibrate, sit back, and enjoy.

☑ Don't ask the person sitting next to you about the reoccurring pain in you back.

☑ When she says her heart is a-flutter, expect her to be examined.

Two actors

- ☑ You're not a guest, you're an extra.
- ☑ Not only will they write their own vows, they'll direct them.
- ☑ Give cash, they never have any money.

Japanese wedding

- ☑ A kimono and a commode are two very different things.
- ☑ Don't feel too bad, you're not the only one who's never seen the bride.
- ☑ Don't worry if you miss this wedding—they'll have pictures.

Nursing-home wedding

- ☑ When they refer to their "little plots of land" they're not talking about building a house.
- ☑ There will only be slow dancing at this wedding (real slow dancing).
- ☑ Here comes the bride. Here comes the bride. She's still coming. Hold on, hold on, she's almost there.

Lis

a second-string bridesmaid

I was a bridesmaid by default—a last minute substitution for an injured bridesmaid.

Friday morning I got a phone call. My friend Laura had just slipped in the shower and broken her leg in two places. An emergency committee elected me to take her place in Gail's wedding party. After picking up Laura's dress at JCPenney's, my boyfriend and I hit the road in order to make it to the rehearsal dinner in Boston that night. We met the groom and all the relatives, and rushed around getting ready for Sunday's service.

What can I say about my bright blue satin dress with puffed shoulders and no discernable waist? My hair blown to beauty parlor heights, a strand of subtle pearls around my neck, and frosted eyeshadow? I looked just like the three other bridesmaids, except the one at the far end who brought her seeing-eye dog to the ceremony.

After the service was over, we left the church, all getting ready to shower Gail and Tom with rice and rose petals. As Gail's father came down the front steps, two policemen came forward and handcuffed him. Without a look at the bride, he turned away, was escorted to the patrol car, and they took off, sirens blaring.

Apparently he hadn't paid alimony or child support in a while and Gail's mother didn't want the opportunity of knowing where he was wasted. She arranged the entire thing.

Which left us with a decision. Did we go bail him out or go to the reception?

Tom, being a thoughtful new husband, offered to get out of the limo, head over to the jail, and meet us at the party. Gail said, no, one drama was enough, and she wasn't showing up at her reception without her groom.

We went to the party, drank like crazy, and hours later, Gail and Tom left for their honeymoon.

I never did find out what happened to her dad. In fact, I never heard from Gail again.

Richard
a willing guest

I was invited to a coworker's wedding and I thought I should go out of obligation. The wedding was nice and the reception was going well until the bride, my coworker, introduced me to her new husband. Our eyes instantly locked and we couldn't stop staring at each other all night.

I thought it was funny and never expected anything to come of it, but when I walked to the back of the reception hall to use the restroom, the groom followed me into the bathroom and locked the door behind me.

He was either going to kick my ass or pinch it, and it turned out that the latter was the case. We fooled around for about half an hour before he had to leave to cut the cake.

on TV

Ally McBeal

How's this wedding scenario? The fiancé's in jail for life and isn't allowed to get married unless he is marrying someone he has children with. Unfortunately for the bride-to-be, she's not pregnant, and he's not allowed to have conjugal visits. A stalemate, you'd think, except for Ally McBeal, who's got a different way of looking at things.

She proposes artificial insemination for her client with sperm from the jailed fiancé. Ally, supportive attorney that she is, even goes to jail with a variety of stimulating magazines, and waits to deliver the sperm while it's still fresh.

After all this organizing, planning, convincing, and hair-flipping, her client decides that love should dictate a wedding, not modern technology.

But the story has a happy ending. The warden relents, allowing the marriage and Ally gets to wear yet another ugly bridesmaid dress as true love wins again.

Mark

a guest with good hands

It seems like most of my adult life is spent hiding in the back of a group of single men all waiting to catch one bride's garter after another. As all of my friends from high school and college got married, it became increasingly obvious to everyone that I was not destined to walk down the aisle. Hell, it became obvious to everyone that I was gay. So when my last friend got married, I decided to be as out as I could be. I talked openly about the man I was dating and even showed a few family members his picture.

I was feeling confident until they announced that it was time for the groom to throw his bride's garter. Suddenly I felt like a kid again, and found myself hiding in the back of a very eager group of single men. You see, the girl who caught the bouquet was an up-and-coming model and tradition dictated that the man who caught the garter not only had to dance with her, but put the garter on her leg—a fate worse than death, I thought, as the groom snapped the garter through the air and right onto the top of my balding head. Everyone began to snicker as I, the gay man, walked up to the model and tried like hell to put the garter on her leg without looking like a complete idiot. Then the snickering turned to laughter as my mother ran around yelling, "He's finally going to get married! My son is finally going to get married, and to such a looker!"

Needless to say, I was humiliated as hell as the model and I walked onto the dance floor. But then the music started: It was a big-band piece. Well, my boyfriend and I had been taking ballroom dancing lessons together, so I thought this would be the perfect time to put all that practice to good work. I twirled, flipped, and dipped that model until the entire audience was applauding. Then for good measure, I grabbed the groom and dipped him as well.

in the movies

The Princess Bride

A lovely young woman, pursued by a prince, falls helplessly in love with a rugged farmboy—no, it's not something on the Playboy Channel, it's a story as old as, well, true love.

The beautiful Buttercup spends most of her adolescence bossing around the equally lovely young farmboy, Westley, who's only response to her is "As you wish." Well, over the years Buttercup learns to love Westley, and why not? He's gorgeous, good with his hands, and only ever says "As you wish" to her—what woman wouldn't fall in love with him? I mean, it's a fairy tale, but it's based in some reality.

Anyway, as reality would have it, Westley is captured by pirates and is never heard from again. Even though she loves Westley, Buttercup agrees to marry the evil Prince Humperdinck for the good of the people (that and the big ol' castle on the hill).

What Buttercup doesn't know is that Humperdinck, along with planning his wedding, is planning on killing his bride, framing his enemy, and starting a war. And you complained about writing thank-you notes on your honeymoon.

But before Humperdinck can put his plan into action, Buttercup is kidnapped by three men—a very smart guy, a hunky Spanish guy, and André the Giant, all of whom also plan on killing Buttercup (poor Buttercup, what did she ever do besides have a really annoying name?).

But before they can have their way with Buttercup, she is rescued/kidnapped by a dark swashbuckler, and we're not talking about his outfit. The fickle Buttercup seems to show an interest in this hero in black (apparently Buttercup is Old English for slut) and admits to him that she's really not in love with the prince. She confides in her kidnapper (much like Patty Hearst), confessing that she actually did love the dead farmboy Westley, but that since he's dead, she had to move on. And to do just that, she kicks the swashbuckler in the face and sends him rolling down the hill.

Mid-roll, she realizes that the handsome man whom she just disfigured with a karate chop is actually the handsome Westley in disguise. In order to check on the damage that she may have done to his face, Buttercup throws herself down the hill and catches up with him.

His beauty still intact, Buttercup declares her love for him all over again, but before they can ride off into the sunset, the prince kidnaps them both. He plans to force Buttercup into a wedding that will suck the life out of her, and then proceeds to literally suck the life out of Westley, with a life-sucking machine.

The day of the wedding, the prince is planning on killing the bride, the bride is planning on killing herself, and Westley is still dead—or is he? No, not even death could stop true love, and with a little help from Billy Crystal, Westley comes back to life and rescues the ever-faithful Buttercup.

True love wins and this beautiful gene pool is guaranteed to go on for generations to come.

Julie
a ravenous bride

My first husband and I planned a huge blowout party for our wedding. Southern Baptists usually don't do that kind of thing but we wanted to do something great to celebrate.

Four days before the wedding, the restaurant we rented called to say they had just changed ownership and the new owners didn't want us to have a party there. After pleading, and a lot of begging and tears, they finally said we could have the room for an hour—no food—no band. So all our friends and relatives stopped by, put presents on a table, and left.

We were starving by the time they all left so my new husband and I, in a tux and a wedding gown, headed for the Hardee's drive-through.

Peggy
a guest on a trip

Nothing interesting happened at any of the weddings I went to. . . . Oh, wait. I was once at a wedding where all the guests poured bowls of macaroni salad onto the dance floor and did the backstroke in it.

That was after we dropped acid.

Does that count?

on TV

The Muppet Show

They are one of television's most famous couples. He, the consummate bachelor; she, determined to be married. He leads with his heart, she is headstrong. He is a frog, she is a pig. Yes, it's the infamous Miss Piggy and Kermit the frog, and while they never got married on television, they did take a walk down the aisle.

The ceremony is beautiful and, in true piggy fashion, everything is just a little overdone. The bride wears white, proving that anyone can wear white at their wedding, and the groom is decked out in a formal tux.

When the priest asks if anyone knows of a reason that this couple can't get married, Piggy cuts him off by muttering under her breath, "Do, it, do it, do it." The flustered priest continues and the overdone ceremony continues without a hitch.

That is, until it comes time for Kermit to take his vows. Instead of saying "I do," he says "I . . . I . . . I want to introduce you to the Amazing Lou Zealand and his live boomerang fish." Suddenly a spotlight goes on, Lou comes out on the altar and fish go flying and then boomeranging back.

In the confusion Kermit ducks out of the ceremony, leaving Miss Piggy stranded at the altar, ducking fish left and right.

in the movies

The Graduate

We have just one word for this movie . . . classic. A classic story and one of the most memorable wedding scenes of all time.

A young Dustin Hoffman has just graduated from college. He finds that he has nothing to do but sit around in his parents pool—well, sit around in his parents pool and seduce their friends. Here's to you, Mrs. Robinson. An older, wiser and sexier Anne Bancroft, dressed in nothing but animal prints throughout the entire movie, has got legs to die for and a wandering eye.

Instead of the usual post-graduation advice, or a lame graduation present, Anne is giving Dustin something he'll remember forever—a sex life. She pops his cherry and goes back for more, not that Dustin is complaining. He's having a great time. But, as most young men who have sex with their parents' friends do, Dustin has to keep his relationship a secret.

Dustin's parents become worried that he isn't getting out much, so they decide to set him up—with Mrs. Robinson's daughter Elaine. Dustin goes out with her, and purposefully acts like a jerk. But like most young girls under the age of thirty, she likes the idea of dating a jerk. And Dustin likes the idea of dating someone who doesn't slather their face in wrinkle cream at night. Dustin's parents are happy with the union as well. The only one, it seems, who is unhappy with the relationship is Mrs. Robinson. And why would she be? After all, a young, able-bodied neighbor boy is hard to train.

Mrs. Robinson tries to break the couple up, but that interference only seems to make the young love blossom even more. Finally Mrs. Robinson threatens to tell her daughter herself, but there is no need, Elaine overhears the conversation, breaks up with Dustin, and goes back to school.

Now Dustin really doesn't have anything to do but sit around the family pool. And one day, while floating on a raft, he comes up with a plan. He's going to go to Elaine's school and stalk her. Remember, this is a younger, happier time— a time when we called it perseverance instead of stalking. (Besides, Mr. Roper is there to protect the girls and a young Richard Dreyfuss is there to call the cops.)

And anyway, Dustin's perseverance doesn't seem to be paying off any more than his stalking. Elaine announces that she is getting married. What's young Dustin to do? Go back to the family pool?

No, in a last-ditch effort, Dustin shows up at the wedding, bangs on the glass doors and gets the girl of his dreams. Without a moment of hesitation, the future Mrs. Hoffman, wearing a traditional white wedding dress and oversized veil, takes one look at the no-name actor she is about to marry, runs out of the chapel, and jumps into Dustin's escape vehicle—a city bus?

Perhaps Dustin's been in the sun too long. Regardless, he's got his tan and he's got his girl. He's also got some explaining to do, especially to the people he's locked in the chapel with a cross. But none of that matters now, as Dustin and his true love ride silently away on the crosstown express to love.

Darryl

a patient guest

A friend of mine from college got married and we all went to the wedding. I barely got to the church before the ceremony started—I sat down just as they started to play "Here Comes the Bride."

Then they played it again.

And played it again.

And again.

And again.

During the fifth or sixth time, one of my buddies got up to see what was happening. He found the bride passed out on the vestibule floor. She had fainted.

But with a little cold water and a couple of slaps (no, only kidding) she was okay and they got married.

Maybe it was a sign she shouldn't have gone through with it. They only lasted eleven months before they split.

Byron
a guest at the closet door

It was a warm August afternoon and my mother and I, along with an awful lot of folks, packed into a big Baptist church to help celebrate our old family friend Tamara's wedding. Her marriage to Reverend Michael was a big deal—relatives, friends, coworkers, and congregants had come to celebrate, some flying in from California, Florida, and all over the South. Tamara was soon going to be a preacher's wife and we all couldn't wait for the ceremony to begin so that we could get to that joyful reception.

Thirty minutes after the ceremony was supposed to start, we were still just sitting there. The church was getting hotter and hotter and everyone started to get antsy. Tamara's maid of honor appeared at the microphone and buzz started traveling through the pews. After several uncomfortable moments she announced that the wedding was not going to take place. Not only did I felt terrible for Tamara, but also for her father, who had spent thirty thousand dollars on a giant wedding reception.

The reverend had sent his best man to tell Tamara that he just wasn't ready for marriage. On hearing this news, Tamara—already feeling faint with nerves and the heat—hyperventilated and passed out. Someone called 911, an ambulance arrived at the church, and Tamara was strapped into the stretcher while still in her wedding dress.

Tamara's sister announced to the stunned guests that the reception would go ahead as planned even though neither the bride nor the groom would be there. There would be plenty of food and drink, a live band, and a DJ. Most of the guests went to the reception but Mom and I didn't go; I thought it would be like tap dancing on someone's grave.

A few days later, my godmother, who had gone to the reception, told me that the hall was packed with guests and everyone danced the night away. Tamara even showed up, sedated, after the hospital released her. She was given a standing ovation and managed to thank people for coming, in between sobbing after every other song.

The guests also heard the real reason the reverend had backed out of the marriage. His male lover had threatened to expose him to the local press if he went through with it. Tamara had never figured it out because she hadn't consummated the marriage and was saving herself for a big wedding night. Incredibly, the reverend appeared before his congregation the next morning and gave a sermon in which he supposedly condemned various assorted sinners.

Tamara has since recovered and has been dating a new guy, although she has no plans to get married anytime soon.

Meg

a bridesmaid taken to the cleaners

I was traveling to Denver for my sister's wedding and tried as best I could to keep my bridesmaid's dress from getting wrinkled. But after an eight-and-a-half-hour car ride, the dress was pretty much a wrinkled mess. We took it to a local dry cleaner and told him we'd be back over the weekend to pick it up.

The rest of the week was busy with wedding events and running around and when I finally got back to the dry cleaner on Saturday morning there was a note saying that he had gone out of town on a fishing trip and wouldn't be back until Monday. Because it was the Fourth of July weekend, the rest of the staff was on vacation and there was absolutely no one who could let me into the store—not the police, the fire department, the better business bureau, or even the mayor's office.

My dress was held captive and my sister's wedding was only four hours away. I called and told her the bad news and she calmly told me to get my ass over to the local Ann Taylor and see if they had another dress just like it.

I got to Ann Taylor, but they were closed as well. Out of frustration and anger I pounded on the door until an employee walked out of the back storage room to see what all the noise was about. Through the locked glass door she told me they were closed for inventory and I told her about the dry cleaning incident. With my hands clasped in prayer and tears running down my face, she invited me in to look for another dress.

They didn't have an identical one in the store, but they did have one in back. She had just boxed it up to send back to the main warehouse and offered to unpack it, alter it, and steam it for me while I waited. I called home to tell everyone the good news, and I got ready for the wedding in the back room of the Ann Taylor while one salesgirl helped me with my makeup and the other sewed me into the dress.

Alex
a fiancé no more

My friend Robin was dying to get married. She busted on her boyfriend all the time to give her an engagement ring.

After months and months, he finally did. Robin wasn't happy with the stone—she thought it was too small and she didn't like the color, so she brought it in to be appraised.

It was a cubic zirconium, not a diamond.

That ended that relationship. She broke up with him on her way home from the jeweler.

Deborah
a bride fit to be tied

I thought I was being left at the altar. My entire family flew from New York to Ireland to see me get married and all they saw was me pacing back and forth and getting more and more angry. My fiancé was almost an hour late for the wedding and I was furious.

I went through the range of emotions: He doesn't love me; he's been in a car accident; he can't find the church. But none of the excuses I could come up with were even close to what really happened. The night before, my fiancé's friends took him out for his bachelor party. Apparently, when all my fiancé's friends got married, they had a tradition of getting the groom really drunk and then trying to embarrass him. As the years went by, they tried harder and harder to outdo one another.

My fiancé was one of the last to get married, and in the name of tradition his friends got him drunk and, after he passed out, they chained him—naked—to a ferry that went back and forth to some of the local islands. They thought someone would free him before the wedding, but it was a rainy day, and not a lot of people were on the ferry. Plus, my fiancé was still passed out, so he wasn't exactly screaming to be freed. I, on the other hand, screamed a lot.

Hayley
a guest with a sweet tooth

My cousin Alison's wedding was pretty uneventful until the cake-cutting ceremony. Two waiters came out with this elaborate wedding cake—at least seven layers, covered with flowers. The cake was on a cart and as the waiters rolled it onto the dance floor, one of the cart's wheels caught the edge of the carpet and the cake went flying.

Most of the cake hit an elderly couple whose backs were facing the bride and groom—they didn't know what hit them. Somehow the tiny top layer survived and, with as much dignity as they could muster, the waiters brought it up for Jeff and Alison to cut.

Grandma Bella insisted that it was bad luck not to serve wedding cake to all the guests so someone in the kitchen had to cut this six-inch cake to serve 250—we were all served a scoop of ice cream with a thumbprint-sized slice of chocolate cake on top.

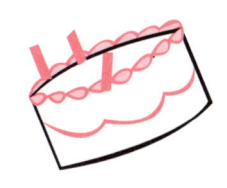

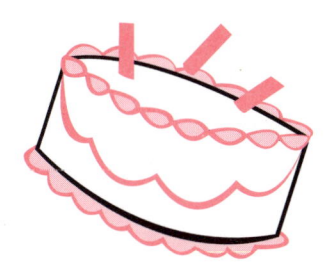

in the movies

Philadelphia Story

A timeless classic that proves nothing is as simple as black and white (even if it's in black and white). . . .

Jimmy Stewart and Ruth Hussey are reporters for a tabloid newspaper—their boss wants to send them to Katharine Hepburn's high society wedding. Her ex-husband, the stunning Cary Grant, has offered to get them into the wedding in exchange for the publisher of the paper not printing a Monica Lewinsky–esque story about Kate's father. Why would Cary care if Kate's father was dragged through the mud? He happens to still be in love with Kate, which is nice for her considering her new fiancé seems to be more in love with her money than with her—money that hasn't helped her parents who, even with all the money in the world, still don't love each other.

Confused?

Well, catch up, because we're only twenty minutes into the movie and the pre-wedding party hasn't even begun. The band is playing, the moon is full, and after cases and cases of champagne, Jimmy Stewart falls in love with Kate; Kate looks like she's fallen in love with him; Kate's Uncle Willie falls in love with Ruth Hussey; Ruth Hussey's jealous of the fact that Jimmy loves Kate because Ruth really loves Jimmy; Cary's at home still loving Kate; Kate's mother falls back in love with Kate's father; Kate's father falls back in love with Kate's mother; Kate and her fiancé fall out of love with each other; and everyone loves Kate's little sister (she's so precious).

With us so far?

By the light of the morning and under the cloud of vicious hangovers, everything seems to come into focus: Kate's fiancé leaves her, Jimmy Stewart asks Kate to marry him; Kate says no and tells Jimmy that Ruth is love with him; Ruth admits her love for Jimmy; Kate's father and mother are still in love; and Kate ends up marrying her ex, Cary Grant, who's always been in love with her.

Drink a lot of champagne while you're watching and you'll understand what we're talking about.

You thought you could never wear it again...

You think your dress was bad . . . While researching this book, we heard about some crazy bridesmaid dresses that are guaranteed to make yours look like haute couture.

Here are four of the worst, and some helpful hints about places you could actually wear them again. And if we can find places to wear these again, *surely* you can find someplace to wear yours.

Winter Wonderland

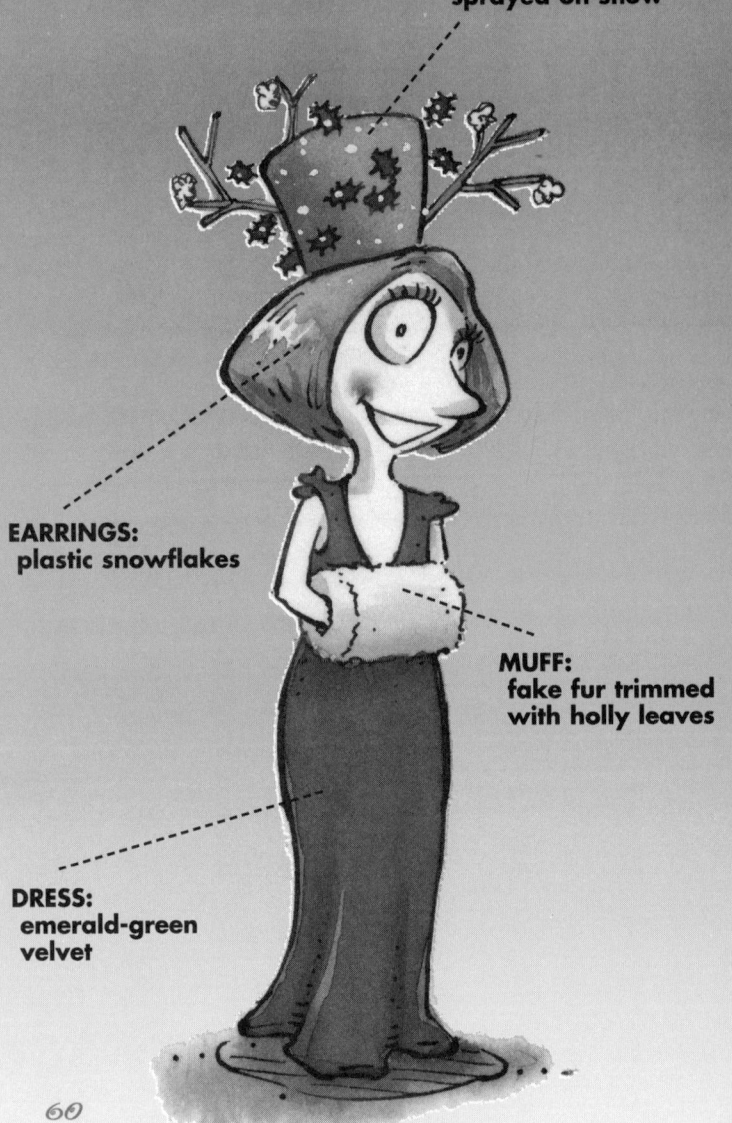

HAIRPIECE: branches covered with sprayed-on snow

EARRINGS: plastic snowflakes

MUFF: fake fur trimmed with holly leaves

DRESS: emerald-green velvet

places you could wear it again

- marching in the Macy's Thanksgiving Day Parade

- hunting in the woods

- greeter at a crafts store

- a backdrop at a portrait studio

- an extra in a local production of *A Christmas Carol*

- frozen in the headlights of an oncoming car

Little Bo-Peep

PARASOL: bigger than the hat

HAT: as big as they could find

CORSET: Scarlett O'Hara tight

GLOVES: elbow-length and pristine white

HOOPSKIRT: as big as they could find

PANTALOONS: lacy and racy

places you could wear it again

- a float in the Rosebowl Parade

- the burning of Atlanta

- greeter at Popeye's Fried Chicken

- storytime at the local preschool

- May Day

- Dollywood

the Studio 54

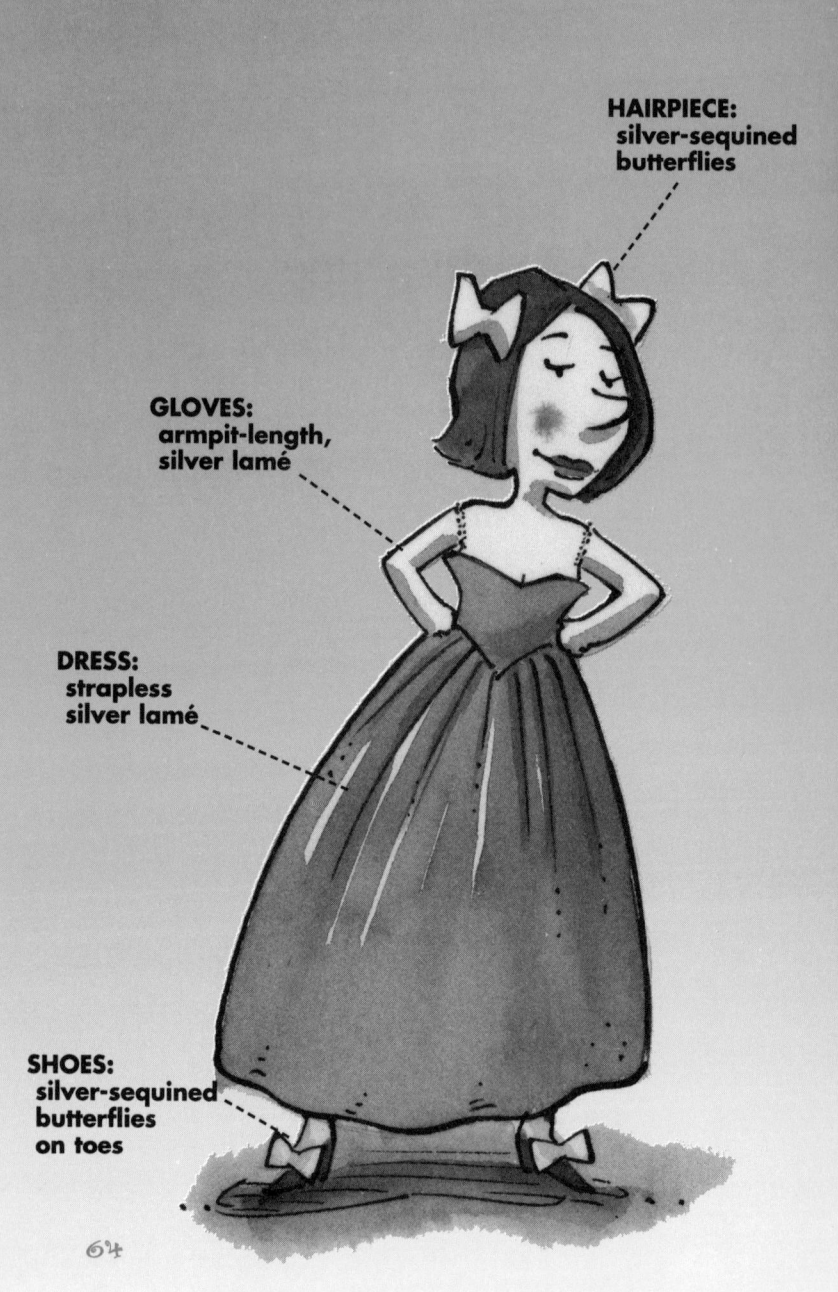

HAIRPIECE:
silver-sequined butterflies

GLOVES:
armpit-length, silver lamé

DRESS:
strapless silver lamé

SHOES:
silver-sequined butterflies on toes

places you could wear it again

- the Copacabana

- NASA test flight

- greeter at a Reynolds Wrap convention

- West Indian Day Parade

- model at a car show

- reflected light source at photo shoots

Bonanza

FLOWERS: lasso woven into bouquet

HAIRPIECE: cowboy hat

DRESS: denim, with leather fringe

SHOES: cowboy boots

places you could wear it again

- extra in a Broadway revival of *Annie Get Your Gun*

- greeter at Wal-Mart

- the O.K. Corral

- rodeo clown audition

- lesbian bar

- tour guide at the Alamo

in the movies

The Wedding Singer

Watching *The Wedding Singer* is a fashion revelation, as in, "Thank God we don't have to wear acid-washed denim, belts that endlessly wrap around your waist, and innumerable rubber bracelets ever again."

There are times when it is hard to follow the plot as we revisited our eighties-fashion faux pas, but the costuming was meticulous—everyone in the movie truly looked the part, except for Drew Barrymore who must have had a clause in her contract stating that she wouldn't have to wear anything eighties.

As for the plot, *The Wedding Singer* is perfect for this book: It covers a host of wedding disasters. Aside from the chronic overuse of hairspray and sequins, there's the wedding where best man, Steve Buscemi, gives a toast mentioning the time he and the groom picked up a couple of prostitutes in Aruba. Adam Sandler is jilted at the altar by his MTV video vixen of a fiancée because he has given up his spandex days. And then there's the highlight of the film: Adam Sandler's virtual breakdown at a wedding reception. Fronting his wedding band and looking like he hadn't slept or taken a shower in weeks, he threatens the bride's father (who, like the rest of the wedding party, is wearing red—yes, red—cummerbunds and bow ties), delivers a soliloquy on the pain of love, and then launches into a searing rendition of

"Love Stinks," serenading all the loser guests. The song ends as the bride's father attacks him, a full-scale battle ensues, and Sandler ends up in the Dumpster.

He also ends up in the dumps, because the new girl of his dreams, Drew Barrymore, is going to get married to someone else. But wait, this is a boy-meets-girl story—she's supposed to end up with Sandler. And true to this plot, Sandler is going to make sure this happens. He hops on a plane to stop Drew's Las Vegas wedding, meets Billy Idol, tells his tale of woe to the entire first-class staff, and then realizes that Drew's actually on the plane.

With Billy Idol's help, he serenades Drew while the stewardess locks her fiancé in the bathroom. Once back on the ground, Sandler gets his girl and a perfect garden wedding. Billy Idol gets his shot at a comeback. And we all get to see how fabulous it is when you fly first class.

Beth
an unfortunate bridesmaid

My sister got married in Washington, D.C., but absolutely had to have a wedding cake from her favorite bakery in Manhattan. As maid of honor, I accepted the responsibility of getting the cake and bringing it safely to the wedding.

The bakery was great: They froze the five layers and packed each in its own box—even writing instructions on how to reassemble it. We bubble-wrapped it, boarded Amtrak with the precious cargo, and headed south.

When we arrived at our hotel, where the wedding was also taking place, I went straight to the kitchen and gave the boxes to the head chef. He put them right into the freezer and guaranteed he would personally take care of the cake the next day.

The next morning, feeling nervous that perhaps the cake wouldn't have enough time to defrost, I ran down to the kitchen to check on it while everyone else was getting dressed.

The chef I had spoken to had called in sick. He left no instructions with anyone about my sister's cake and no one else in the kitchen knew what I was talking about. I went straight to the freezer to get the boxes, but they weren't there. My heart started pounding. We tore the kitchen apart—but the cake was nowhere to be found. I got hysterical. The wedding coordinator called a local bakery with an emergency order for a replacement cake.

When it came time for the cake-cutting ceremony, everyone gathered around to see the fabulous tiered cake from Manhattan that my sister had been talking about for weeks. Instead, we got a chocolate sheet cake with white frosting and pink letters.

on TV

Rhoda

Mary Richards's most famous friend finally has it all: a good job, a sitcom of her own, and a man to spend the rest of her life with—that is, if she survives the wedding.

The headstrong Rhoda decides to get married by a judge in a low-key ceremony. But her even more headstrong mother (Nancy Walker of "quicker-picker-upper" fame) has other plans. Unbeknownst to Rhoda, her mother has planned an entire wedding with food, flowers, a wedding dress for Rhoda, and friends from *The Mary Tyler Moore Show*.

The entire gang is there for the weekend wedding festivities, which include flashbacks of some of Mary's and Rhoda's worst dates ever.

But all those dates are nothing compared to the disaster of her wedding day. Phyllis forgets to pick Rhoda up, and Rhoda finds herself running through New York in her wedding dress and a cardigan sweater, trying to find a taxi.

Desperate, Rhoda finally heads into the subway, makes her way uptown to her parents' house, and into her husband's arms. Unfortunately all that effort was for nothing: Neither the wedding nor the sitcom lasted very long.

Doug

a stranded groom

My fiancée and I decided to circumvent any kind of wedding/family craziness and get married in Hawaii. We planned a beautiful sunset wedding on the beach in Kauai and had everything all set to go when we arrived.

The morning we left New York, a hurricane blew in and as we flew west, Kauai was being devastated. The pilot kept the passengers updated—we had a stopover in Texas and no one knew if we'd be able to get to our final destination or not.

We couldn't. We arrived in Hawaii to find that no one was allowed to travel to Kauai—they had no electricity, no plumbing, no resources. So we now had to plan our perfect wedding all over again. We had two days to find a photographer, a videographer, someone to perform the ceremony, a location, a bakery to make us a vegan wedding cake, and a place for our honeymoon.

Dealing with my family would have been slightly easier.

Steve

a guest with flair

My cousin was getting married and asked my younger brother if he would be the ring bearer. My brother was incredibly excited about the prospect of getting dressed up and walking down the aisle, but when he found out his sister was going to be the flower girl, he wanted her job.

We tried to tell him that boys can't be flower girls, but he was having nothing to do with it. We all thought he'd get over it before the wedding, but right before the ceremony started, he informed us that he still wanted to be the flower girl and was not walking down the aisle unless he had a basket of flowers.

The organist started playing "Here Comes the Bride" but my brother wouldn't let her pass. My cousin was furious and on the verge of killing him when her quick-thinking father grabbed two calla lilies from a flower arrangement in the back, slipped one ring onto each stem, and sent my happy brother off down the aisle.

Today, my brother and his boyfriend run a flower shop. I swear to God.

in the movies

When Harry Met Sally

When Harry met Sally it was on a car ride from the University of Chicago to New York City. They had both just graduated, and decided to carpool into their future. On the road, Harry hit on Sally, but she couldn't sleep with him because he was dating a friend of hers. She did tell him however, that she would like to just be friends. (How many of us have been blown off with that line?) But Harry wasn't going to fall for it. He told her that men and women couldn't be just friends because the desire for sex always got in the way. So rather than sex getting in the way, they decided to part ways.

The next time Harry met Sally was on a plane—five years after they had parted in New York, and Harry's on the brink of getting married, much to Sally's surprise. His theory is that after sex, the first thing men think about is how long do they have to hold the woman before they can go home. Apparently Harry has just given up, and decided to hold Helen, his fiancée, all night. Sally has definitely given up on Harry and again they part ways.

The third time Harry met Sally was in a bookstore. Another five years have passed and Sally is sure that Harry wouldn't remember her, but remember her he does. They go out to lunch together and talk about their failed relationships. Sally and Joe have just broken up and Harry is headed for divorce.

After they console each other, they become friends. Their friendship is solidified in a montage that shows New York at it's most beautiful and Meg Ryan and Billy Crystal at their funniest. Then, to insure that they will always remain friends, Harry and Sally introduce each other to their respective best friends. Harry sets Sally up with Bruno Kirby and Sally sets Harry up with Carrie Fisher. Harry doesn't like Carrie and Sally isn't too taken with Bruno, but Bruno likes Carrie, Carrie likes Bruno, and at the end of the dinner, they hop into a cab and into each other's arms.

It seems that love is in the air, because Bruno and Carrie move in with each other, and Harry and Sally have sex. Yes, sex. Sally finds out that her ex is getting married, Harry comes over and, yadda yadda yadda. Well, he spends the night, leaves first thing in the morning, and by that evening, they both decide that it was a mistake, but it's too late. It's out there . . . sex.

Harry and Sally drift apart, but they are brought together by Bruno and Carrie's wedding. Sally is the maid of honor and Harry is the best man. She's in a green taffeta dress with a plunging black velvet neckline, he's in a tux and they're both in the kitchen fighting when Bruno and Carrie give their toast—perhaps the most embarrassing wedding toast ever. *"To Harry and Sally—if Marie or I found either of them remotely attractive, we wouldn't be here today."*

And what's to find attractive? They're both behaving very badly. But after a month of reflection, Harry has an idea why. He's in love. And like a three-year-old who hits a girl to show his affection, Harry runs across town (who can find a cab on New Year's Eve?) to hit Sally with the news.

And boy does it hit her. She cries. She complains. She whines. And it's not about the electric-blue, strapless, rhinestoned dress she's wearing. But in the end she realizes she's in love too and three months later they get married, with a fabulous coconut cake—chocolate sauce on the side.

Stephen
a ring bearer on a mission

When I was a very small child, I was the ring bearer at my aunt's wedding and my cousin Maria was the flower girl. Even at an early age I was a stickler for rules, and I became really upset when my cousin refused to sprinkle her flower petals.

As we walked down the aisle, I tried to encourage her to throw the flowers, but she refused. I even tried to grab a handful and throw them myself, but she pulled away too quickly.

Finally, I got so upset that I dropped the pillow with the rings on it and tackled my cousin halfway down the aisle. I left her sobbing, grabbed her basket and dumped all the petals right at the foot of the altar.

The ceremony didn't start for another twenty minutes until Maria's father finally got her to stop shrieking.

Diane
a bridesmaid on the fringe

I don't like weddings.

I don't like having people look at me.

I don't like wearing anything that's not black.

I fought as hard as I could about being a bridesmaid at my cousin Mary's wedding but I had no choice, so I spent one hellish Saturday night in a peach, strapless gown with a giant tulle skirt, a bow in my hair, and pumps dyed to match (I feel sick just saying that).

When I couldn't take any more, I whispered to my horrified mom that I was leaving. I grabbed my black hightops and leather jacket from her car and headed to New York City.

I got to Manhattan and headed down to CBGB's, a club in the East Village. Some guy doing a sound check asked me if he could autograph my dress. He pulled a fat black marker out of his bag and scrawled right across the peach skirt. My dress and I were the performance art of the night—by the time I left, my dress was completely covered.

I got home at five the next morning, put my peach-and-black dress in a plastic bag, and left it at the curb for the garbage man to pick up. It was definitely not a dress that I'd wear again.

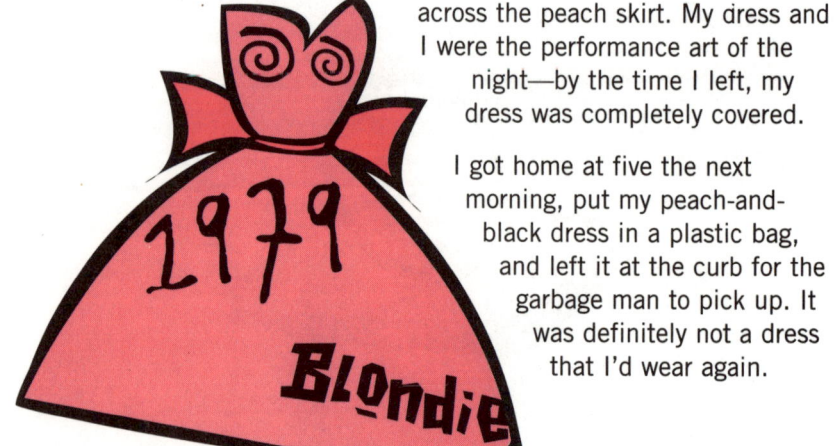

Deb

a tired bride on the move

We found a great apartment to move into after we got married. The only problem was that my current landlord had rented my apartment out from under me. He told me on Friday afternoon I had to be out by Monday. And my wedding was Sunday.

Perry, my fiancé, and I packed all day Friday, renting a U-Haul on Saturday morning to move all my stuff. By the time we were done loading the truck, getting to the new place, and unpacking, it was four in the morning and we were in the middle of a huge disaster.

An even bigger disaster was that the wedding was at eleven and I couldn't find my dress. We searched for over an hour before it turned up. Perry left and I finally crashed, on a box spring, at five-thirty.

We had to get up extra early to return the U-Haul. At 9:00 A.M. Perry arrived in a tux and, with me in my wedding gown, we drove to the truck-return center. Then we finally headed for the church.

As I got out of the car, I realized that I never put on my wedding pumps, so I got married in a pair of white tennis shoes. Fortunately my dress was long enough to cover them in most of the photos.

on TV

Friends

Poor Ross. His first wife leaves him for another woman and he has to attend their wedding.

Then he destroys his next chance at happiness when he mentions the wrong girl's name before they get to "I do." Emily, his very proper British bride, finishes the ceremony, walks back down the aisle, and quickly disappears out a bathroom window, nowhere to be found. After countless phone calls, dozens of roses, and out-and-out begging, Emily shows up at the airport to go on their honeymoon, only to find Rachel, the old girlfriend whose name Ross mentioned, happy to go to Greece in her place. Emily runs, Ross runs after her, and Rachel spends two weeks in a honeymoon suite on the beach by herself.

Ross returns to New York to find he has lost his apartment, his wife is unreachable, and he has to move into an apartment inhabited by ducks, BarcaLoungers, Joey, and Chandler. On the other hand, he gets to live across the hall from Rachel. Thoughts, anyone, on where this is going?

Lisa
a city guest at a country wedding

One of my friends got married to a guy from Nebraska, and they decided to have a country wedding. The bridesmaids all wore jean skirts and the groomsmen all wore black cowboy hats and gun holsters. The bride rode in on a horse and you could smell the barbeque from the awaiting picnic reception.

Now, I'm from Manhattan, so this is all a little strange to me, but what I thought was really strange was when the priest asked if anyone knew why this couple couldn't get married—the groom and the bride's brother pulled their guns from their holsters and popped off a round of caps before the brother faked his death right there on the altar.

Ann
a frustrated bride

As I walked down the aisle, gazing at my husband-to-be, I saw that he was sweating profusely, pale white, and shaking. I thought it was just nerves—but no, it was the flu.

He spent the reception sitting by himself in the corner.

When we got to the elegant, wonderful hotel we were spending our wedding night in, he soaked in a hot bath, ordered soup from room service, and was asleep by 9:00 P.M.

Not exactly the evening I had planned.

in the movies

Muriel's Wedding

An entire movie dedicated to weddings and set to an ABBA soundtrack. If you can walk down the aisle in synch to "Dancing Queen," then you could have been a bridesmaid in *Muriel's Wedding*.

This black comedy starts off with Muriel catching the bouquet at her friend's wedding. She then catches the groom and one of the bridesmaids, still in coral tulle and rhinestones, having sex. As if that wasn't enough, she's escorted out by the police for wearing a way-too-tight leopard print ensemble, which, by the way, was stolen—and that's all in the first five minutes.

Like all young Australian girls, Muriel's under the impression that if she gets married she'll instantly become a different, better person, and, like all young Australian girls, Muriel is going to be prepared. After stealing all of her parents' money, going on a long vacation, moving to Sydney, changing her name to Marial, and getting a job in a video store, Muriel/Marial spends her free time running to every bridal shop in town, trying on wedding dresses, and then having polaroids taken to show her imaginary, hospitalized, cancer-ridden mother.

Eventually her hard work pays off and our girl finds someone who'll marry her—too bad he's a South African Olympic swimmer who's more interested in a green card than a wife.

Still, the wedding will make Marial happy, and the money his family is paying the bride will go a long way toward paying her parents back.

On the big day, Marial, looking better than she ever did in one of those Sydney bridal shops, comes bounding down the aisle to ABBA, while her bridesmaids, in tan tulle, quickly follow. The ensemble passes the gaping mouths of the baffled onlookers and practically runs over the stunned groom, who's wondering if a gold medal is worth all this.

The vows are exchanged, the rings are put on, and the reality of a loveless marriage sets in. Marial now spends her day watching the videotape of the wedding, hoping to recognize that happy, ABBA-go-lucky-girl in all that white sateen.

In the end, Marial realizes that she doesn't need a man to make her happy (score one for Gloria Steinem) and decides that she's not going to settle for a loveless marriage. She also changes her name back to Muriel—recognizing that she doesn't really want to become a completely different person, (score one for Freud), just a better version of the person she already is: a person who's going to marry for love but still loves the thought of getting married—that and ABBA.

Ida
a bride who left her mark

I ordered a beautiful wedding dress from Bonwit's, only it never showed up. In a last-minute panic, I borrowed a dress from a friend of mine at work. When I picked it up the day before the wedding from the dry cleaners, I was horrified to find that the finish had come off the buttons running down the back of the dress—all one hundred of them.

The next morning after I got dressed, my aunt put white shoe polish on each and every button to cover up the black. I didn't tell anyone what had happened, but I noticed that every time I danced with someone, they'd walk away with white smudges on their hands and head quickly to the bathroom.

Heather
a bride minus one

One of my best friends never showed up at my wedding.

She was arrested after my bachlorette party, for driving under the influence and harrassing a police officer. They threw her in jail, and with all the wedding craziness going on, no one was around to get her phone call and bail her out.

At least she wasn't one of my bridesmaids.

Carolyn

a stubborn bride
with an even more stubborn mother

Fruit cup. Pale slices of acidy grapefruit and blanched maraschino cherries. Everyone serves it. No one eats it. So why was this little cup of acid indigestion causing me to break out in hives? Because for some reason it became a huge bone of contention between my mother and me.

She wanted to serve it—I didn't. I told her it was tacky; she said it was tasteful. I told her it left a bad taste in one's mouth; she said it was a nice way to cleanse the palate. I told her the fruit cup alone would cost us eight hundred dollars extra; she said she'd pay it.

In the end, I won. There would be no fruit cup at the wedding. Of course my mother wasn't speaking to me that day, but it didn't matter—I had won at least one of my many wedding battles.

I proudly sat down for the beginning of dinner, upon which the waitress served me a huge punch bowl of fruit cup. I glared at my mother, who spoke her first words of the day to me: "I didn't do it."

It turns out that my father arranged for the waitress to serve me—and me alone—the fruit cup. He thought it would be a good way to break the ice between me and my mother.

I have to admit it worked. I smiled widely at my mother as I pushed the bowl in front of her.

Liz

a bride in search of a bathroom

We wanted to do something different for our wedding so we planned to have it out in a scenic mountain range in Northern California. To get to the site you had to drive over a mountain and into the valley—little did we know that our wedding weekend was during the local annual pumpkin festival—traffic was so bad that many of the guests were over two hours late.

The wedding site was rustic, a nice way of saying no indoor plumbing. They had Portosans, but there was no way I was using one while in my big white wedding dress. Because we had to hold off on starting the ceremony (my fiancé's parents were among the late arrivals), I desperately had to go to the bathroom. Needless to say, I had my period and had to go squatting in the woods to change my tampon. I did a pretty impressive job of keeping my dress clean, but you can definitely see a ring of dirt and dried leaves in all the pictures.

on TV

Seinfeld

It was the wedding that was never meant to be.

George proposes to Susan only because Jerry is getting engaged. When Jerry changes his mind at the beginning of a new season, George is stuck, and no matter how hard he tries or how desperate he gets, he can't get out of getting married.

The wedding is approaching, the season is ending, and there is no hope in sight. The invitations are ordered and George, getting in one last shot at being himself, has Susan order the cheapest envelopes the printer has. Lucky for him, the glue is toxic; she passes out, and dies.

He's free. Free at last. Free to dance down the hospital halls. Free to pursue Marisa Tomei. However, after he finds out how wealthy Susan was, and how, as just her fiancé, he gets nothing, he has a momentary twinge of disappointment, but let's get real—George as a rich man? No, better that he comes back the next season as the loser that we love.

in the movies

My Best Friend's Wedding

In college, best friends Michael (Dermot Mulroney) and Jules (Julia Roberts with her trademark 1980s hair) made a rather desperate pact: If neither one was married by the time they turned twenty-eight, they'd marry each other (like twenty-eight is so old).

Nine years later, and two months before Jules's twenty-eighth birthday, Michael calls, desperate to talk. Remembering their pact, she thinks he's calling to propose. But before she can let him down easy, Michael drops a bomb—he's getting married to blond bombshell Kimmy.

Michael pleads for Jules to come to the wedding and hold his hand, but she has other plans. She's got four days to split up the happy couple and make Michael fall in love with her—this is where the scheming, conniving, and the bitchiness begins.

The moment Jules lands, the ever-so-perky Kimmy (played by the ever-so-perky Cameron Diaz) makes Jules her maid of honor and shrouds her in a form-fitting lavender dress designed to make the other, fatter bridesmaids weep into their taffeta.

Jules tries everything she can to break up the couple, but this seems to be true love. At her wit's end, she calls on her friend, the all-too-handsome and all-too-gay George (Rupert Everett) for help. George flies to town to support Jules, but before he can sing a show tune, Jules has told everyone that she and George are about to be married. Then George does sing a show tune and flies back to New York beseeching Jules to tell Michael the truth.

She doesn't (that would be the end of the movie and we still have forty-five minutes to go). Instead, Jules uses her fake marriage to George to get Michael jealous. It works. Michael almost tells her he loves her, but the words don't come easily and the moment passes. And for the groom-to-be it was just that, a moment. But Jules isn't going to lose that easily—she once and for all sabotages the couple and the marriage is off.

The day of the wedding, Michael goes to Kimmy's to reunite and Jules runs after him. Jules kisses Michael and Kimmy catches them. Kimmy runs away, Michael chases her, Jules chases him and then calls George, who aptly points out that no one is chasing Jules.

Jules finally catches Michael and comes clean, telling him that she sabotaged the marriage and vows, and that she'll find Kimmy and get her to the church on time (poor Jules, these are the only vows she'll be taking today).

Jules finds Kimmy and the two have a catfight in the women's bathroom of Wrigley Field. Kimmy wins and gets the man (horribly barbaric, but fun to watch). The ceremony is beautiful and the reception is stunning. Jules looks fantastic in her form-fitting lavender dress, and the other two bridesmaids sing a beautiful song to the newlyweds while outfitted in horrific, floral-printed cabana dresses. The happy couple pulls away in a white Rolls-Royce while sparklers line the driveway of their mansion—thus proving that when it comes to a great wedding reception, there is no substitute for money.

But don't feel too bad for Jules—the all-too-handsome George is there for the rescue, and while there will be no sex between them, there will be a lot of dancing. And besides, why would Jules want to marry a sportswriter who's on the road all the time, when she can dance with an incredibly handsome gay man who knows that lavender is not purple, notices how beautiful her skin is, and can fix her hair if, God forbid, it should ever frizz?

Greg

an overexposed guest

At my friend Bob's wedding they had disposable cameras on all the tables. By the end of the night, we were all trashed and taking stupid photos of one another.

When the bride's mom got them developed, we all found out how crazy they really were. One of the guys had taken a camera into the bathroom and shot half a roll exposing himself.

He exposed himself even more than he thought he did. He was the only person at the wedding wearing a brown suit and so he kind of identified himself on film.

The bride's mom called his mother and his girlfriend. Harsh.

authors

Elissa Stein is a mother, runs her own graphic design business, and still finds time to work on offbeat projects.

Her first two books, *Tales from the Prom*, and *Chunks: A Barfology* are beginning to carve a thin niche on bookshelves everywhere.

She lives with her husband Jon and daughter Isabel in the West Village and regrets that her bio is not as funny as Daniel's.

Daniel Mailliard is an associative creative director for a New York advertising agency. Daniel's first book, *Tales from the Prom*, made his mother more proud of him than any of her other kids.

With several short stories published, Daniel is thrilled to be working on his second book with Elissa, and has been starting his Great American Novel for the past two years.

thanks

The authors would like to thank Jon Lichtenstein for occassionally laughing with us, our families for always bearing with us, Dana Albarella for fighting for us, Chris Murphy for working with us, and Jennifer Herbert, for taking care of us.